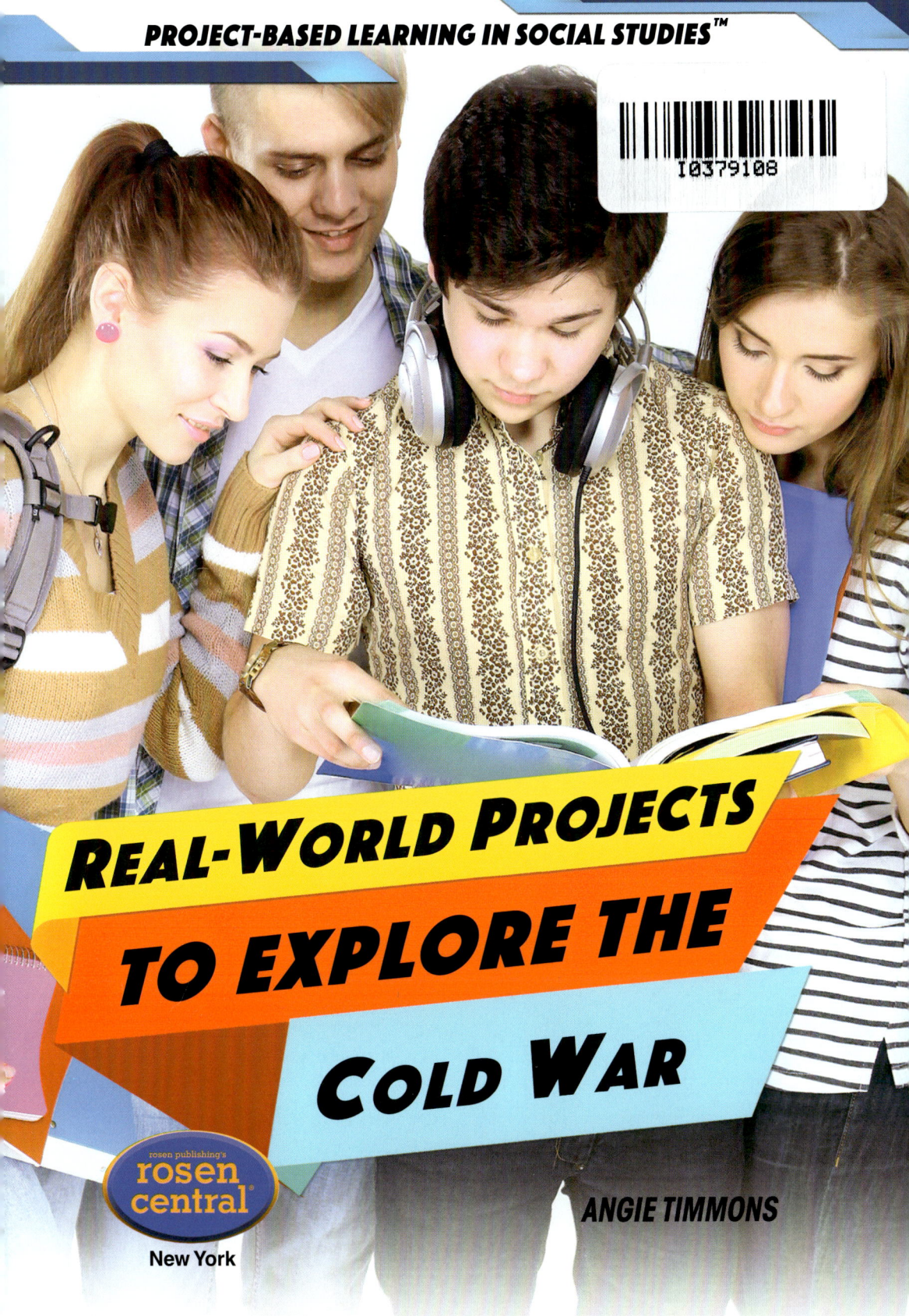

PROJECT-BASED LEARNING IN SOCIAL STUDIES™

REAL-WORLD PROJECTS TO EXPLORE THE COLD WAR

ANGIE TIMMONS

Rosen Publishing's Rosen Central
New York

Published in 2019 by The Rosen Publishing Group, Inc.
29 East 21st Street, New York, NY 10010

Copyright © 2019 by The Rosen Publishing Group, Inc.

First Edition

All rights reserved. No part of this book may be reproduced in any form without permission in writing from the publisher, except by a reviewer.

Library of Congress Cataloging-in-Publication Data

Names: Timmons, Angie, author.
Title: Real-world projects to explore the Cold War / Angie Timmons.
Description: New York : Rosen Publishing, 2019. | Series: Project-based learning in social studies | Includes bibliographical references and index. | Audience: Grades 5–8.
Identifiers: LCCN 2017050755| ISBN 9781508182160 (library bound) | ISBN 9781508182177 (pbk.)
Subjects: LCSH: Cold War—Problems, exercises, etc. | World politics—1945–1989—Problems, exercises, etc.
Classification: LCC D842 .T56 2019 | DDC 909.82/5—dc23
LC record available at https://lccn.loc.gov/2017050755

Manufactured in the United States of America

CONTENTS

Introduction 4

Chapter One: The Roots of
the Cold War 9

Chapter Two: A Clash of Systems . . . 25

Chapter Three: The Tools of
the Cold War 33

Chapter Four: The Events of
the Cold War 44

Glossary 56
For More Information 57
For Further Reading 59
Bibliography 60
Index 62

INTRODUCTION

For four decades, the Soviet Union (also known as the Union of Soviet Socialist Republics, or USSR) and the United States shadowboxed, feinting and striking on a shadowy stage of world politics. Rather than meet on the battlefield, the two superpowers fought through covert operations and espionage, secret pacts and alliances, and suspicious whispers of subversion. This protracted battle was the Cold War, a forty-four-year conflict that divided the world along ideological lines and physical border walls.

At midnight on November 20, 1989, the Cold War and Soviet Union began to crumble along with the Berlin Wall, which had separated communist East Berlin (in East Germany) from West Berlin (in West Germany) for twenty-eight years. Thousands celebrated the wall's destruction as, for the first time in nearly thirty years, West Berliners could finally welcome their East Berlin counterparts over the wall. As they hacked

INTRODUCTION

When border restrictions relaxed between East and West Berlin in November 1989, Berliners and visitors chiseled souvenirs from the wall that had defined their existence for decades.

down the wall with any tool they could find, Berliners from both sides of the wall mixed in "No-Man's Land," the area on each side of the wall in which many East Berliners had been shot attempting to escape to West Berlin.

Erected in 1961, the Berlin Wall was just one of many points along the border that separated the Soviet-led, communist Eastern Bloc and the Western world. Because more than two million East Germans fled west as the Eastern Bloc moved closer to isolation, Soviet-sympathizing East Germany built the Berlin Wall to shut down access to the West.

After four decades of isolation and war, Soviet leaders began a political discourse with Western powers—many of whom had been Soviet allies in World War II—in the late 1980s. These renewed relationships, combined with international pressure and internal problems, resulted in the Soviet Union's dissolution and its re-entry into the global society.

The Cold War is one of history's most fascinating periods, and Project-Based Learning, or PBL, is a great way to learn the nuances of a complex conflict that defined four generations. In a conflict as layered as the Cold War, traditional methods of teaching like lectures and the study of thick textbooks are unlikely to make many details stick with learners. Project-Based Learning puts students in charge of how they learn. Using PBL, students engage with subject matter over an extended period through investigation, dynamic group collaboration, decision-making and problem-solving, reflection, and public presentation. PBL asks students to frame subject matter within a real-world context by tying areas of study to current events and personal concerns. Instead of asking students to sit still

INTRODUCTION

and memorize huge chunks of information, PBL sends students on their own journey to understand the Cold War and its lasting impacts.

PBL encourages the use of multiple technologies. As learners move through the various stages of a PBL project, they are challenged to find diverse and innovative ways to find, store, and organize their research and to take a multifaceted, technology-based approach to designing an end product for public presentation. One goal of project-based learning is to prepare students for real-world demands. Modern-day students and employees must possess more than mere skills or knowledge. They must be able to take initiative and ownership for projects and assignments, organize using a diverse array of programs, solve problems independently, collaborate and communicate well, and present to an audience. As technology allows us to connect globally, the modern workspace is increasingly virtual. These new developments demand an enhanced ability to take responsibility and orchestrate work with little to no supervision. Project-based learning encourages the use of technology that helps students research, organize project assets and research, collaborate, and create products of all kinds—all skills necessary for your future. Rely on various tools available to store your information, share with your group members and teachers, and create an end product. Endeavor to use collaborative tools that you and your team are able to access outside of school, as your project may involve homework.

Following is a list of some helpful project-based learning applications. All of them are free, offer free subscriptions, or

have free trial versions.
- **Research:** Britannica School, Google, especially Google Scholar, Todoist, EndNote, Digital Public Library of America, Citelighter, SweetSearch, Diigo
- **News:** CNN Student News, Newseum, KQED, PBS Newshour Extra, Smithsonian's TweenTribune
- **Organization, Collaboration, and Communication:** Stormboard, Google Drive and Hangouts, Evernote, Pinterest, Livebinders, Slack, Asana
- **Mind & Concept Mapping:** Mindomo, Mindmeister, MindMup
- **Posters, Multimedia, and Publishing:** Glogster, Issuu, Scrivener
- **Digital Presentation/Project Portfolios:** Pathbrite, Google Slides, PowerPoint, PresentationTube, Prezi
- **Website creation/blogging:** Google Sites, Wikispaces, WordPress, Weebly, Wix, Duda, SnapPages, Yola, Sitey, StudentShow
- **Video:** YouTube, iMovie, LifeLogger, WeVideo, Magisto, TeleStory
- **Animation, Drawing, and Infographics:** Do Ink, Piktochat, Typrorama
- **Podcasts:** GarageBand, Audacity
- **Survey/Feedback:** Survey Monkey, Google Forms.

While the Cold War is a fascinating chapter in history, its secretive nature and complicated web of participants make it a difficult study. PBL removes much of that difficulty and adds in an interdisciplinary approach that puts students in the driver's seat.

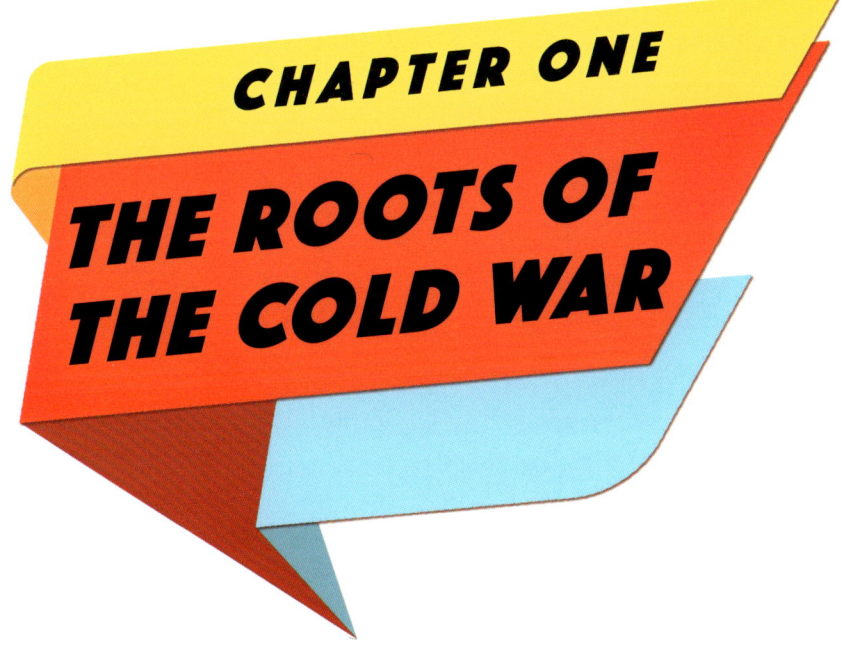

CHAPTER ONE
THE ROOTS OF THE COLD WAR

In August 1945, the United States simultaneously ended World War II and redefined warfare by dropping two atomic bombs on Japan, killing about 150,000 people instantly.

The atomic bombs were the first nuclear weapons ever used. To this day, they remain the only use of nuclear weapons in a war. The sheer scale of destruction and loss of life that the bombs caused forced Japan to surrender to the United States and its allies, the Allied Powers, in September 1945—four months after Japan's Axis Powers ally, Germany, had surrendered.

Exhausted and depleted from six years of war, living in a newly post-nuclear world, and struggling to rebuild nations decimated by war, World War II's victors stumbled into a shadowy conflict that turned one-time allies into enemies and lasted an astonishing forty-four years: the Cold War.

Question: What Makes a War Cold?

In October 1945, English author George Orwell penned an essay in which he pondered the new world, post-atomic bomb. Orwell theorized that nuclear weapons would give rise to a state of permanent war between superpowers that would one day be, like the United States already was, capable of nuclear warfare. In this permanent war, these superpowers would let the mere threat of nuclear attack bring weaker, poorer nations to heel.

Orwell called this state of affairs, in which powerful nations were made invincible by the mere ability to threaten their global neighbors with nuclear attacks, a "cold war." By 1947, the term "Cold War" gained traction after its mention by writers and political leaders around the globe.

Throughout the Cold War, Western nations—led by the United States—sustained an open rivalry against the Soviets and their allies in the Soviet Bloc. Despite its duration, the Cold War lacked large-scale, direct fighting between its combatants. As the only nation proven to possess nuclear capabilities at the Cold War's start, the United States had the threat of nuclear attack to hold over the heads of enemies. Though the Soviet Union clearly had hostile intentions toward the United States and other Western powers, it couldn't launch a large-scale attack against the West until it, too, had nuclear weapons. While the Soviet Union raced to develop nuclear arms, words became one of the Cold War's most powerful weapons. Cold War-era speeches, frequently written by speechwriters who worked behind the scenes, gave rise not only to certain terms that defined the conflict (such as "Star Wars," Evil Empire," and "Iron Curtain"), but to the conflict itself.

THE ROOTS OF THE COLD WAR

The British novelist, essayist, and journalist George Orwell called the new threat of nuclear war a "cold war" in which the threat alone would keep nations in a state of unrest.

PROJECT
THE WORLD TURNS COLD

Speeches delivered by Cold War leaders were designed to provoke an emotional response from their audiences, serve as a rallying cry for everything from peace to all-out war, or provoke enemies. Many Western and Soviet leaders came and went during the war's forty-four years, and with each new leader came a new style of rhetoric.

As a team, attempt to solve problems of the past by writing speeches for key Cold War figureheads who would have had the power to influence a course of events for the better. Rather than provoking each other or rallying the public to support violent aggression, try to write speeches aimed at preventing specific tragic or otherwise significant Cold War events.

- The project group should choose two or three Cold War events that might have been prevented or scaled back if the leaders in power at the time had chosen different words and different actions.
  - An internet search will yield many Cold War timelines and information on the period's most significant events.
- Select one of the events you researched to focus on. Write a speech for a leader in power

THE ROOTS OF THE COLD WAR

when the event occurred (for instance, a speech to about the Berlin blockade should be written for US president Harry S. Truman or Soviet premier Joseph Stalin).
- In writing the speech, consider what could have been done to prevent the negative outcomes of the events the group selected.
  - What alternative strategies could leaders have employed to right the course of history?

Project-based learning encourages students to work as a team to solve problems—even problems from the past, like those that caused and influenced the Cold War.

- What verbal or physical attacks could they have refrained from to avoid what actually happened?
- What hard lines did these leaders take that could have been softened to prevent heightened or prolonged hostilities?

• Choose one group member to deliver the group's speech to the class. The speaker will deliver the speech while playing the role of the Cold War leader for whom it was written.
- To that end, the project team should review real-life speeches delivered by the leader from whose point of view the speech was written and note the leader's manner, tone, and style.

• After the speech, share with the class how and why the group picked the event and leader it did. As a class, discuss how the course of history might have been changed if Cold War leaders had used a problem-solving approach rather than a problem-causing approach.

> **QUESTION: HOW DOES THE FATE OF BERLIN ENCAPSULATE THE COLD WAR AS A WHOLE?**

The Soviet Union invaded Berlin in April 1945 and waged the Battle of Berlin, which led to Hitler's suicide and Germany's surrender. World War II in Europe ended in the same

THE ROOTS OF THE COLD WAR

In April 1945, Soviet soldiers swarmed war-torn Berlin. The Battle of Berlin lasted seventeen days, forced Germany's surrender, and gave the Soviets a stake in Berlin's future.

city where it had begun, and the fate of Germany and most of Europe was in the hands of the Allied Powers. Following Germany's surrender, Germany, Austria, and their capital cities—Berlin and Vienna—were divided into four occupation zones, each controlled by one of the main Allied nations (Britain, France, the United States, and the Soviet Union). Berlin was in a desperate state by the time the Allied leaders divided it up. The city had been destroyed by the war, and the return of millions of Germans who had lived in German-occupied lands catapulted Berlin into a precarious state of hunger and disease.

World War II dramatically impacted geographic territories, boundaries, and societies across Europe, not just in Berlin. In July 1945, Soviet Premier Joseph Stalin, the new US President Harry S. Truman, and outgoing British Prime Minister Winston Churchill (who was replaced in late July by Clement Attlee, the victor in Britain's July election) gathered in Berlin to discuss the defeated nations' future in a meeting called the Potsdam Conference. The conference lasted through early August and yielded plans for post-war Europe.

By the time of the Potsdam Conference, Stalin knew through a network of Soviet spies in America that he'd been excluded from his allies' plans for the atomic bombing of Japan (which would happen in August 1945). Stalin refrained from confronting his allies about this. Instead, he focused on making sure that the agreements that had been made earlier that year at the Yalta Conference earlier in the year stayed in place.

THE TOOLS OF THE COLD WAR

intelligence on a closed-off society like the Soviet Union was no easy task.

PROJECT
SPIES IN YOUR SCHOOL?

After the Cold War ended, civilians and government agents alike came forward with their stories. Former covert agents, writers, and journalists took up the pen to tell real-life spy tales. Research the information available to uncover the lives and missions of Cold War spies. For this project, practice in-person, real-life Cold War-era spy techniques in front of the class.

The CIA spent the Cold War spying on the United States' enemies—namely, the Soviet Union.

- *Research Cold War espionage. Find out how spies obtained, conveyed, and delivered information, what impact their intelligence had on Cold War operations, and how they stayed in the spy game without getting caught—as well as what happened if they were caught.*

- *After learning about Cold War-era espionage, research present-day spy activities around the globe. Some questions to get you started:*
  - *What are some notable recent examples of government espionage?*
  - *How is modern-day spying different from Cold War spying? (Hint: look to the internet.)*
  - *How do countries gain access to other nations' intelligence?*
  - *How do we know anything about closed-off societies such as North Korea?*
- *Put together a presentation of what you learned for you class. Incorporate spy techniques where you can.*
  - *Find places in plain sight in the classroom to make dead drops of information you learned.*
  - *Develop ways to communicate using a code or signals that only those in the know can understand.*
- *On presentation day, use techniques like signals, disguises, encrypted messages, and dead drops planted in the classroom or in areas of the school approved for the project's use. See if anyone can crack your code.*
- *Come out of the shadows! Once the espionage presentation is done, come together as a class to discuss the present-day spy activities you researched. The discussion should include thought-provoking questions, such as:*

THE TOOLS OF THE COLD WAR

On both sides of the Iron Curtain, Cold War intelligence gathering resulted in major innovations, such as sound amplifiers that helped agents spy on enemies.

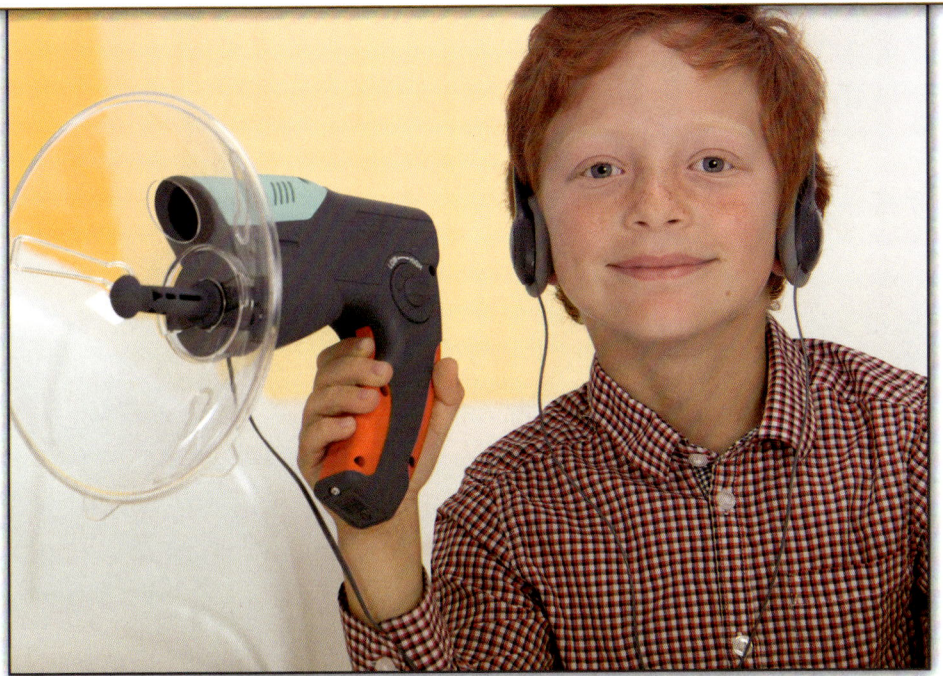

- *Do you believe spying on other countries is useful?*
- *Do you believe spying is moral?*
- *Now that you know more about Cold War espionage, how does that knowledge affect your views on present-day spying?*
- *If you were a top government official, what would you do with sensitive intelligence about another country?*

> QUESTION: HOW WAS PUBLIC OPINION MANIPULATED IN THE COLD WAR?

Propaganda was an extraordinarily powerful tool in the Cold War. Without battles and mass casualties to bolster public support of the prolonged conflict, the United States and the Soviet Union both relied on propaganda to maintain public loyalty.

A CAMPAIGN OF FEAR

Between 1947 and 1956, Senator Joseph McCarthy engaged in a tireless effort to root out communists in the Second Red Scare, a campaign that spread fear of communism among Americans. (The First Red Scare in the United States happened in early twentieth century after the Bolshevik Revolution in Russia.) His targets spanned from everyday citizens to Hollywood stars to high-level government officials. McCarthy's allegations gave rise to congressional committees, such as the House Committee on Un-American Activities, dedicated to uncovering and punishing communists in the United States. Laws, arrests, and repression efforts swept the nation. These measures, eventually known as McCarthyism, met with little resistance. Early Cold War-era anti-communist initiatives were popular, despite their violations of constitutional rights.

Capitalizing on an already-fearful American public, McCarthy convinced the nation that communist subversives lurked in every shadow. Anyone who disagreed with him was instantly branded un-American or a possible communist spy.

THE TOOLS OF THE COLD WAR

Under the guise of free speech, patriotism, and national security, efforts like the Second Red Scare spread anti-communist propaganda across the United States. The rise of television in the 1950s gave the government an entirely new delivery system and a captive audience for anti-communist messaging. The Soviet Union went even further. Behind the Iron Curtain, the Soviet government controlled all aspects of life: food, utilities, and even the words people read, heard, and spoke. The Soviet government had near absolute control of the messaging

Propaganda was used to reach out to the public on both sides of the Cold War. This Soviet propaganda promises to expose the anti-Soviet plans of "imperialists" and religious groups.

its public consumed. That messaging, of course, was primarily anti-American, anti-Capitalist propaganda.

PROJECT
INSTILLING FEAR BY ANY MEANS AVAILABLE

Develop a propaganda campaign designed to spread fear among the public about another country. Obvious choices in the modern era are nations like Iran and North Korea, due to the Cold War-like nuclear tensions with those nations.

- *Research Cold War-era propaganda on both sides of the conflict. Investigate the types of media employed to spread propaganda, whom that propaganda targeted (especially children), the messaging contained in Cold War propaganda and how it changed over time, and the fate of anyone who deviated from Soviet messaging.*
- *Using a combined approach that includes both Cold War-era propaganda media (such as posters, advertisements, pamphlets, and films) and modern media (such as blogs, social media, podcasts, etc.), create propaganda materials.*
- *After distributing the propaganda materials to your class, discuss it with your classmates. Talk about the moral implications of manipulating people through propaganda and the dangers*

THE TOOLS OF THE COLD WAR

In project-based learning, students take the lead in developing a project based on a central question or idea. This is usually done with the help of a team or group.

of propaganda in today's super-connected world. Discuss how the proliferation of media and technology has impacted the way people view the world. With blogs, Twitter accounts, and podcasts mixed in with legitimate news, how can people tell what's fact and what's fiction?

- Discuss what might have happened if Cold War leaders had the technology available today, such as Twitter. With the power to constantly deliver propaganda, would a nuclear war have happened? Is it possible today's technologies are making us (or the people in any other nations) easily manipulated?

> **QUESTION: HOW DID THE COLD WAR LEAD TO INNOVATION AND THE DEVELOPMENT OF NEW TECHNOLOGIES?**

In their quests to outdo each other, the United States and the Soviet Union engaged in a rigorous competition to produce superior scientific and miltary products. The Soviet Union's closed society status meant neither the Soviets nor the Americans had access to the other's latest technologies. Because of this, spy technology grew. We owe certain technologies—including digital cameras, digital file sharing, and the internet—largely to Cold War spying.

Some Soviet-American competitions were more public, however. One example is the Space Race to put a human on the Moon. The Americans won that contest on July 20, 1969, when astronauts Neil Armstrong and Buzz Aldrin became the first people to walk on the Moon. However, it was the Soviets who had been the first to launch a person into space. Cosmonaut Yuri Gagarin achieved that goal on April 12, 1961.

PROJECT
COLD WAR INNOVATION

The Cold War spurred innovation in many fields. Most items were designed for the military or espionage community, but a lot of them ended up having broader uses.
- *Do research on five different technologies that were developed during the Cold War.*

THE TOOLS OF THE COLD WAR

One of the many Cold War innovations was stealth technology. The F-117 Nighthawk, pictured here, was developed in the early 1980s and was the first plane built with such technology.

- Note why each technology was developed, what need it filled, and who used it.
- Also note any unexpected uses of the technology that later developed.
- Using a digital presentation and actual props (model rockets, toy military planes, digital cameras, etc.), conduct a presentation about the texhnology that interested you the most.
- Conclude the presentation with a discussion about the pros and cons of the technology you profiled in your presentation. For instance, a pro might be that America put a man on the moon, while a con might be that defense spending was often at the expense of other programs, such as education.

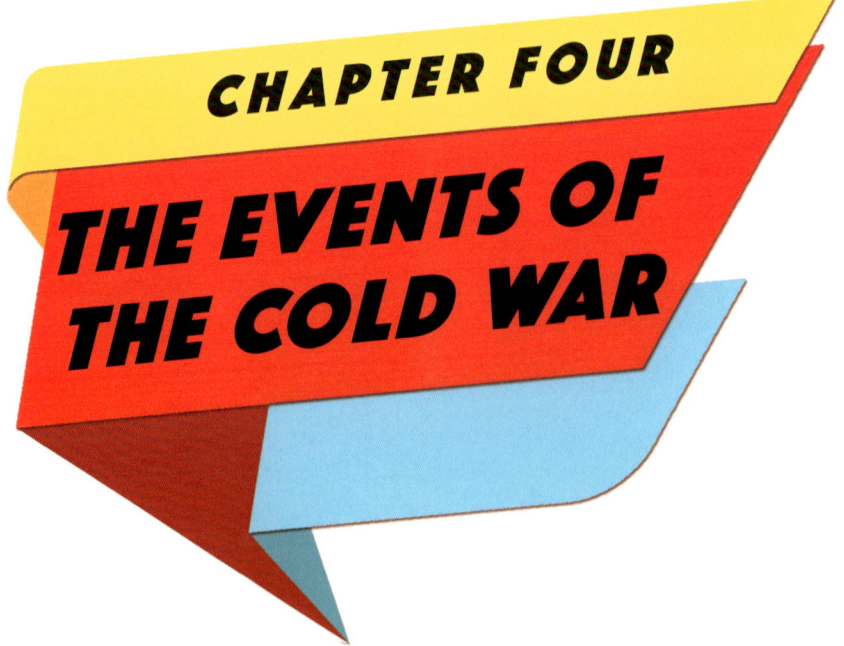

CHAPTER FOUR

THE EVENTS OF THE COLD WAR

There were a few moments, such as the Cuban Missile Crisis, when it looked like war might actually break out between the Soviets and the Americans. For the most part, though, the Cold War drudged on in the shadows and the United Stated and the Soviet Union sought to gain footholds in developing nations, primarily in the Middle East, Africa, and Latin America. For more than four decades, the United States and the Soviet Union calculatedly backed dozens of nations, revolutions, and violent conflicts around the globe, hedging their bets on efforts that may be advantageous to their positions. Both superpowers used unrest in distant countries to indirectly wage war against each other. One notable example is the Vietnam War, a nineteen-year conflict that was wildly unpopular with the American public and enormously costly, both in terms of resources and human life.

QUESTION: WAS THE COLD WAR ACTUALLY THE THIRD WORLD WAR?

THE EVENTS OF THE COLD WAR

US and South Vietnamese troops gather to discuss movements during the Vietnam War, one of many proxy wars through which the United States and Soviets indirectly fought each other.

People often wonder if there will ever be a World War III. Some historians and political analysts believe society has progressed past the societal ills that caused the two world wars. Others believe global conditions are ripe for a third world war that could be the deadliest one yet. Instead of asking if there will ever be a World War III, ask this: did World War III already happen?

The Cold War is notable for its lack of open hostilities. Compared to the wars that preceded it, the Cold War as we commonly think of it—a power struggle between the communist Soviet Union and Western powers, specifically the United States—was not a direct conflict. What's missing from this equation, however, is the staggering number of deadly conflicts related to the Cold War. For example, troops from the US and other Western nations fought—and tens of thousands died—in wars against communist (though not Soviet) forces in Korea and Vietnam.

THE KOREAN WAR

When World War II ended with Japan's surrender in 1945, the United States and Soviet Union entered Japanese-held Korea. The Soviets accepted the surrender of those north of the 38th parallel in Korea, while those south of the 38th surrendered to the Americans.

Within a few years, the Soviet Union had installed a communist dictatorship and strong military in North Korea. North and South Korea were effectively two separate nations. In 1950, North Korea declared war on South Korea, wanting to unite all Korea under one communist government.

Facing this new communist threat in North Korea (which was aided by communist China and the Soviet Union), anti-communist powers such as the United States deployed forces to fight North Korea alongside South Korean forces. A bloody war was waged for three years.

It was the first time that the United States and the USSR indirectly fought each other by using other nations as their battlegrounds. A ceasefire was called in July 1953, but hostilities never ended. North Korea is still an insular, secretive nation, following the lead of Cold War-era communist nations. North Korea poses an ever-increasing nuclear threat, casting a Cold War shadow on modern day diplomacy.

The United States persisted in Vietnam for years, driven primarily by the desire to defeat the side backed by the Soviet Union. Like many Cold War conflicts in which the Americans and Soviets were involved, the Vietnam War was wasteful, held ambiguous significance, and was ultimately a useless venture in the pursuit to expand global influence.

PROJECT
COLD WAR NEWS

Acting as a wire service for major news outlets in the Cold War era, test the theory that the Cold War was in fact a third world war. Develop a brief news transmission for each global conflict related to the Cold War, beginning with the 1945 Berlin blockade and ending with the dissolution of the Soviet Union in 1991.
- *Work in a small team. Each member should handle a unique news wire. Transmissions only need to contain a couple of sentences. Much like an emergency alert on a cell phone, these mock news wires are intended as alerts, not full news stories.*
- *The wire transmissions can take many forms, such as emails, recorded audio, tweets, and*

text blasts. Make sure all the transmissions are permanently recorded in one central place that team members can access anytime, anywhere, such as a Google doc the team members update with each transmission they send.
* After the team's final transmission from 1991 is dispatched, review the central document where the team noted each transmission. Based on the number and nature of the trans-

Using modern electronic messaging, such as Twitter or texting, is a good way to quickly share a significant amount of information with your group and other peers.

missions, debate whether the third world war already happened.
- *Present to the class by sharing examples of the wire transmissions. Reveal the list of Cold War-related conflicts the mock news wire service had to transmit. Share the team's thoughts on whether or not the Cold War was really World War III.*

QUESTION: HOW DOES THE CUBAN MISSILE CRISIS COMPARE TO CURRENT-DAY TENSIONS OVER NUCLEAR ARMS?

The 1962 Cuban Missile Crisis was a standoff between US president John F. Kennedy and Soviet premier Nikita Khrushchev over Soviet plans to install nuclear missiles in Cuba. What followed was more than a year of hostilities between the United States and the Soviet Union—the Cuban Missile Crisis.

In Cuba's new president, Fidel Castro, Khrushchev saw an ally in the West, where Khrushchev hoped to expand communist ideals and practices. Castro admired communism, was located close to the United States, and was blatantly anti-American.

To keep communism out of the West, the Americans backed a mission to oust Castro through a covert operation called the Bay of Pigs Invasion in 1961. On April 15, American B-26 planes bombed four Cuban airfields. On April 17, 1,500 Cuban dissidents—trained by the CIA in Guatemala and supplied with US weapons—landed at Cuba's Bay of Pigs. The operation failed, but led Cuba to request nuclear weapons

US president John F. Kennedy met with pilots who flew reconnaissance missions over Cuba, gathering intelligence on the Soviet missile bases that sparked the Cuban missile crisis.

from the Soviets to protect itself from any further attempts at invasion by the United States.

On October 14, 1962, American spy planes took photos of what CIA analysts soon identified as Soviet missile bases. Over the following weeks, tensions between the Americans and Soviets came to a peak, with the United States establishing a blockade to stop Soviet ships and an American spy plane shot down above Cuba. Khrushchev and Kennedy sent letters back and forth, eventually coming to an agreement in which the Soviets removed the missiles in Cuba, the Americans withdrew missiles from Turkey and Italy, and a nuclear hotline was set up between Moscow and Washington to make it easier for leaders to communicate during times of crisis.

THE EVENTS OF THE COLD WAR

PROJECT
THE NUCLEAR LEGACY

With current nuclear threats from nations like Iran and North Korea, some historians believe the Cold War's nuclear legacy is alive and thriving. To explore this notion, create a multiepisode podcast that explains the Cuban missile crisis in detail. Your podcast should also open discussion about the Cold War's nuclear legacy.

- Research accounts from the Cuban missile crisis era (newspaper articles, first-hand accounts, declassified government documents, and news reels from the US, Soviet, and Cuban sides of the Crisis).
    - *Where does the Cuban missile crisis leave the United States, Cuba, and Russia today?*
- Research the Cold War's nuclear legacy. Consider questions such as:
    - *What nuclear programs exist today that didn't before the Cold War, and how are they used?*
    - *Why are nuclear programs and weapons still a concern after all these years, considering they haven't been used since 1945?*
    - *Who are the major players in the present-day nuclear landscape?*
    - *What recent events remind you of the Cuban missile crisis?*

- Research current nuclear issues. Issues to consider include:
  - The 2015 agreement that curbed Iran's nuclear program.
  - Iran's claim that its nuclear program is peaceful and not intended for warfare.
  - President Donald Trump's actions in existing nuclear agreements, and what impact those actions may have.
  - North Korea's refusal to engage about the extent of its nuclear arms program.

Researching history and current events for project-based learning helps project groups develop accurate presentations and final products. Research can be done on an individual basis or as a team.

THE EVENTS OF THE COLD WAR

- *North Korea's parade of ballistic missiles in Pyongyang in 2015.*
- *North Korea's many nuclear missile tests in 2017, including several aimed at Japan.*
- *Plan a radio show-style podcast that is at least three episodes long. Choose topics for your podcast episodes, and outline what you plan to discuss in each one. Then record the episodes. Try to include parts of speeches from the Cuban Missile Crisis or other audio clips.*
- *Play your podcast for your entire class. Follow it with a class discussion of today's issues.*

QUESTION: WILL THE LESSONS OF THE PAST PREVENT ESCALATION OF THE NEW COLD WAR, OR IS HISTORY DESTINED TO REPEAT ITSELF?

While the Cold War eventually ended in the Soviet Union's breakup, it is difficult to declare a "winner." Like many of the conflicts that raged during the Cold War era, the era's conclusion leaves a whiff of uncertainty. The Western world's checkered history with the Soviet Union has left an uneasy relationship with Russia. Current events speak to the "New Cold War," a shadowy, often invisible, and hard-to-track conflict with unseen aggressors. The New Cold War is fought online, where Russia is alleged to have made targeted, malicious attacks against the United States' Democratic Party and interfered with the 2016 US presidential election. For years, Russia has harbored Edward Snowden, a formal federal employee who leaked classified information about the United States online. Russia's refusal to turn Snowden over smacks of old Cold War rivalries.

Run by former KGB agent Vladimir Putin, Russia became the subject of harsh criticism in the 2010s due to its restrictive and intolerant policies. In making homosexuality illegal, present-day Russia seems to be borrowing some of the Soviet Union's old policies of repression.

Russian president Vladimir Putin sparked international controversy when he refused to extradite American Edward Snowden to the United States.

In 2014, Russia invaded and annexed the Ukrainian territory of Crimea. This led to unrest across the region and strained Russia's diplomatic relations with other world leaders. The present-day struggle with new power dynamics, inexperienced or unpopular world leaders, and Russia's seeming return to repression and aggression are almost uncanny parallels to the conditions that defined the Cold War.

PROJECT
INTERNET INTRIGUE

Espionage and intelligence gathering has moved online, giving rise to a whole new generation of spies and investigators. Develop a presentation to educate others about the threat of cyberwarfare.

Research how Russia has used the internet to spy on or destabilize other countries. Look for articles online, in newspapers, or in magazines. Find at least five articles from the last six months and at least five articles that are over six months old. Questions to consider include:

- *What is the relationship between the Russian government and the teams that carry out online attacks on its behalf?*
- *What kinds of attacks have the teams used?*
- *What countries or international groups have been the targets of Russian attacks?*
- *How have Western intelligence organizations traced the attacks back to Russia?*

- **Put together a presentation outlining what you have learned. Conclude your presentation with an internet literacy primer to help your audience recognize the results of Russia's "troll army" if they encounter it online.**
  - *Include examples of the ads that Russian agents placed on social media sites such as Facebook in 2016.*
  - *Offer tips that people could use to spot Russia-sponsored messages.*
- **Make your presentation to your classmates. Ask for additional suggestions on how to spot and alert others to Russian influence online.**

GLOSSARY

atomic bomb An explosive bomb powered by the release of energy as the result of the splitting of nuclei from a heavy chemical element in a rapid chain reaction.
capitalism An economic system of private or corporate ownership of capital investments.
combatant A person or country fighting in a war.
communism An economic, political, and social theory that advocates the elimination of private property, and in which all goods are owned communally.
covert Not openly shown or admitted to by the responsible party.
cyberwarfare Conflict that takes places over computers and computer networks, such as the internet.
dissident A person who speaks out against a government and its policies.
dissolution The coming apart of something.
espionage Spying or using spies to obtain classified and secret information about foreign governments.
ideology Motivating beliefs.
propaganda Ideas, facts, allegations, and rumors spread to deliberately further a cause and damage an opposing cause.
rhetoric The art of, or tools used in, persuasive speaking.
socialism Various economic and political theories that include collective or governmental ownership and administration of goods and their production.
suppression Crushing or putting an end to something.
total war An unrestricted war in which the laws of war regarding weapons, territories, targets and combatants, as well as objectives, are generally disregarded.

FOR MORE INFORMATION

Central Intelligence Agency (CIA)
Office of Public Affairs
Washington, DC 20505
(703) 482-0623
Website: www.cia.gov
Facebook: @Central.Intelligence.Agency
Twitter: @CIA
The CIA offers archives, publications, and declassified information related to the Cold War—both from the American and Soviet perspectives.

Cold War Museum
PO Box 861526
Vint Hill, VA 20187
(540) 341-2008
Website: museum@coldwar.org
The Cold War Museum is a charitable organization that aims to not only educate about the Cold War, preserve Cold War-related assets and information, but also to promote Cold War research.

Hoover Institution
434 Galvez Mall
Stanford University
Stanford, CA 94305
(650) 723-1754
Website: hooverpress@stanford.edu
Facebook: @ HooverInstStanford
Twitter: @HooverInst
The Hoover Institution's Archives of the Soviet Communist Party and ad Soviet State collection offers more than 11,000 microfilm reels related to political conditions in the Soviet Union from 1903-1992.

Library of Congress
101 Independence Ave, SE
Washington, DC 20540
(202) 707-5000
Website: http://www.loc.gov
Facebook: @libraryofcongress
Instagram and Twitter: @librarycongress
The Library of Congress offers archives and exhibits on a diverse range of historical events, including the Cold War. Its "Revelations from the Russian Archives" offers a Soviet perspective on the Cold War—an interesting

National Archives
8601 Adelphi Road
College Park, MD 20740
(866) 272-6272
Website:
   https://www.archives.gov
Facebook: @usnationalarchives
Twitter: @USNatArchives
The United States' National Archives allows the world a look at the nation's history through documents, records, and photos, providing an excellent source for primary documents.

Veterans Affairs Canada
PO Box 7700
Charlottetown, PE C1A 8M9
Canada
(877) 604-8469
Website: http://www.veterans
   .gc.ca/eng
Facebook: @CanadaRemembers
Twitter: @VeteransENG_CA
This government agency serves and necessary perspective to consider when studying any international conflict. the veterans of Canada's armed services, including those who took part in Cold War conflicts, such as the Korean War.

Vietnam Veterans Memorial
5 Henry Bacon Drive NW
Washington, DC 20002
(202) 426-6841
Website: https://www.nps.gov
   /vive/index.htm
Facebook and Twitter:
   @NationalMallNPS
This National Parks Service site honors the veterans who served in the Vietnam War. It features a wall with the names of the more than fifty-eight thousand service members who died in the conflict.

FOR FURTHER READING

Curley, Robert. *Spy Agencies, Intelligence Operations, and the People Behind Them.* New York, NY: Rosen Publishing, 2013.

Day, Meredith. *The Cold War.* New York, NY: Britannica Educational Publishing, 2017.

Grant, R.G. *The Cold War.* London, UK: Encyclopaedia Britannica, Inc., 2012.

Harasymiw, Therese. *How Do I Use a Library?* New York, NY: Rosen Publishing, 2015.

Hoffman, David E. *The Billion Dollar Spy.* New York, NY: Doubleday, 2015.

La Bella, Laura. *How Do I Use a Database?* New York, NY: Rosen Publishing, 2015.

Lucas, Edward. *The New Cold War: Putin's Russia and the Threat to the West.* New York, NY: St. Martin's Press, 2014.

Maxim, Bailey. *The Post-Cold War World.* New York, NY: Rosen Publishing, 2017.

Murphy, John. *Socialism and Communism.* New York, NY: Rosen Publishing, 2015.

Rosen Publishing Group, Inc. *Personal Freedom & Civic Duty.* New York, NY: Rosen Publishing, 2014.

Segal, Adam. *The Hacked World Order: How Nations Fight, Trade, Maneuver, and Manipulate in the Digital Age.* Philadelphia, PA: PublicAffairs/Perseus Books Group, 2016.

Trenton, Russel. *The Russian Revolution: The Fall of the Tsars and the Rise of Communism.* New York, NY: Rosen Publishing, 2016.

Wallenfeldt, Jeff. *The Growth of a Superpower: Documenting America: The Primary Source Documents of a Nation.* New York, NY: Rosen Publishing, 2013.

BIBLIOGRAPHY

Boss, Suzie. "Twenty Ideas for Engaging Projects." George Lucas Educational Foundation, September 12, 2011. https://www.edutopia.org/blog/20-ideas-for-engaging-projects-suzie-boss.

Buck Institute for Education. "About BIE." Retrieved September 8, 2017. http://www.bie.org/about. "Capitalism." *World Geography: Understanding a Changing World,* ABC-CLIO, 2017.

Churchill, Winston. "The Iron Curtain Speech" (speech, Westminster College, Fulton, Missouri, March 5, 1946). https://www.cia.gov/library/readingroom/docs/1946-03-05.pdf.

CNN Cold War: Relive History. "The Cold War." CNN. 1998. September 30, 2017.

"Communism." *World Geography: Understanding a Changing World,* ABC-CLIO, 2017. September 7, 2017.

Educational Technology and Mobile Learning. "Must Have Rubrics for Integrating Project Based Learning Activities in Your Class." May 25, 2014. http://www.educatorstechnology.com/2014/05/must-have-rubrics-for-integrating.html.

Ferenz, Kathleen. "Project-Based Learning with Primary Sources." *Library of Congress Teaching with Primary Sources.* Library of Congress, 2010. http://www.loc.gov/teachers/tps/quarterly/project_learning/article.html.

Fogarty, Richard. "Cold War." *World Geography: Understanding a Changing World,* ABC-CLIO, 2017.

History.com. "Cold War." Retrieved September 8, 2017. http://www.history.com/topics/cold-war.

Hoffman, David E. The Billion Dollar Spy. New York, NY: Doubleday, 2015.

"Marxism." World Geography: Understanding a Changing World, ABC-CLIO, 2017. Retrieved September 9, 2017.

John F. Kennedy Presidential Library and Museum. "Thirteen

BIBLIOGRAPHY

Days in October." Retrieved November 26, 2017. http://microsites.jfklibrary.org/cmc.

Nemchenok, Victor V. "In Search of Stability Amid Chaos: US Policy Toward Iran, 1961–63." Taylor & Francis Online, February 25, 2010. http://www.tandfonline.com/doi/abs/10.1080/14682740903178579.

Riley, Susan. "Are You Using Projects or Project-Based Learning?" Education Closet, April 14, 2016. https://educationcloset.com/2016/04/14/using-projects-project-based-learning.

Smith, April. "Driving Questions in Project-Based Learning." Performing in Education. Retrieved September 8, 2017. https://performingineducation.com/2017/03/driving-questions.html.

TeachThought Staff. "A Project-Based Learning Cheat Sheet for Authentic Learning." TeachThought, August 2017. https://www.teachthought.com/project-based-learning/project-based-learning-cheat-sheet-authentic-learning.

Tierney, John J., Jr. "Cold War Geopolitics: Containment." The Institute of World Politics, March 3, 2016. https://www.iwp.edu/news_publications/detail/cold-war-geopolitics-containment.

Tucker, Kristine. "Cold War Project for High School." Classroom. Retrieved September 9, 2017. http://classroom.synonym.com/cold-war-projects-high-school-8269084.html.

World History Project. "Cold War Timeline." Retrieved September 7, 2017. https://worldhistoryproject.org/topics/cold-war.

INDEX

A
Aldrin, Buzz, 42
Allied Powers, 9, 16, 17
  "Big Three" leaders, 17
annexation, 17, 20
Armstrong, Neil, 42
atomic bomb, 9, 10, 16
Attlee, Clement, 16
Austria, 16
Axis Powers, 9

B
Baltic countries, 17
Bay of Pigs Invasion, 49–50
Berlin, 16, 18
  Berlin Blockade, 13, 47
  Berlin Wall, 4–6, 18
  East Berlin, 4–6
  invasion of, 14
  occupation of, 18
  West Berlin, 4–6
blog posts, 8, 22–24, 40–41
Bolshevik Revolution, 38
bourgeoisie, 27
Britain, 16, 17, 27, 33, 34

C
capitalism, 25, 27, 30
Churchill, Winston, 16, 17, 20
CIA, 34–35
class struggle, 27
communism, 5, 25–27, 28, 30,
  31–32, 38, 46, 49
Communist Manifesto, The, 27
Cuban missile crisis, 44, 49–50,
  51, 53

D
debate, 28, 31–32, 49

E
Eastern Bloc, 6, 20, 22, 34
Engels, Friedrich, 27
espionage, 33, 34, 35–37, 42, 54–55

F
feudal system, 27
figureheads, 12
foreign intelligence, 33, 34
France, 16
free trade, 30

G
Gagarin, Yuri, 42
Germany's surrender, 14–16
global superpowers, 25, 44

H
Hitler, Adolf, 14, 17
House Committee on Un-American
  Activities, 38

I
Iron Curtain, 10, 20–21, 22–24, 39

J
Japan, 9, 16

K
Kennedy, John F., 49, 50
KGB, 34, 54
Khrushchev, Nikita, 49, 50
Korean War, 46–47

INDEX

M
Marx, Karl, 26, 27
McCarthy, Joseph, 38
McCarthyism, 38
Mexico–United States border wall, 24
MI6, 34

N
National Security Act, 34
North Korea, 36, 40, 46–47, 51–53
nuclear hotline, 50
nuclear warfare, 9, 10
nuclear weapons programs, 33, 51

O
Orwell, George, 10

P
philosophers, 27–29
Poland, 17
postwar Europe, 17
Potsdam Conference, 16, 17
project-based learning, 6–8
proletariat, 27
propaganda, 33, 38–39, 40–41
Putin, Vladimir, 53

R
Reagan, Ronald, 32
Red Scare, 38, 39
Roosevelt, Franklin D., 17

S
satellite states, 20
Snowden, Edward, 53
socialism, 31, 56
Socialist economies, 30
Soviet allies, 6, 10, 18, 22
Soviet Bloc, 10
space race, 25, 42, 43
speeches, 10, 12–14, 20, 29, 53
spy techniques, 35
Stalin, Joseph, 13, 16, 17, 32
Stasi, 34

T
technology, 7, 33, 41, 42–43
Truman, Harry S., 13, 16, 34
Trump, Donald J., 52
Twitter, 41, 47

U
United Nations, 17

V
Vietnam War, 44–47

W
World War II, 6, 9, 16–17, 20–21, 25, 45–46
  alliances, 17, 18–19
  end of, 14
  postwar landscape, 25
World War III, 44–46

Y
Yalta Conference, 16, 17

ABOUT THE AUTHOR

Angie Timmons is a writer who studied journalism and sociology at Texas Tech University. After a few years in news writing, she worked as a technical writer and content manager for software and communications companies in Dallas-Fort Worth. She currently works as a marketing writer for a housing developer. Her other titles for Rosen include *The Nanjing Massacre*, *Everything You Need to Know About Racism*, and *How to Create Digital Portfolios to Show What You Know*. She lives in a Dallas suburb with her husband, Jason, and their three cats.

PHOTO CREDITS

Cover, p. 1 By SL_Shutterstock.com; p. 3 Ollyy/Shutterstock.com; p. 4 Pressmaster/Shutterstock.com; p. 5 Mirrorpix/Getty Images; p. 11 adoc-photos/Corbis Historical/Getty Images; p. 13 Rawpixel/Shutterstock.com; p. 15 Alexander Ustinov/Hulton Archive/Getty Images; p. 19 Encyclopaedia Britannica/Universal Images Group/Getty Images; p. 21 Peteri/Shutterstock.com; pp. 23, 41 Monkey Business Images/Shutterstock.com; p. 26 Everett Historical/Shutterstock.com; p. 29 Wavebreakmedia/iStock/Thinkstock; p. 32 Dirck Halstead/The LIFE Images Collection/Getty Images; p. 35 Saul Loeb/AFP/Getty Images; p. 37 Lea Paterson/Science Photo Library/Getty Images; p. 39 Heritage Images/Hulton Archive/Getty Images; p. 43 Digital Storm/Shutterstock.com; p. 45 Hulton Archive/Archive Photos/Getty Images; p. 48 Syda Productions/Shutterstock.com; p. 50 Bettmann/Getty Images; p. 52 wavebreakmedia/Shutterstock.com; p. 54 Alexander Nemenov/AFP/Getty Images.

Design: Nelson Sá; Layout: Raúl Rodriguez; Editor: Amelie von Zumbusch; Photo Researcher: Sherri Jackson